What ! You need a laptop for your studies?

Wouter Fouche

Published by Wouter Fouche, 2025.

WHAT ! YOU NEED A LAPTOP FOR YOUR STUDIES?

First edition. September 18, 2025.

ISBN: 979-8232358914

Written by Wouter Fouche.

What Everybody Needs to Know Before Buying a Laptop to Use for Study

By Wouter Fouche

• • • •

INTRODUCTION: MORE Than Just a Gadget

These days, we see children as young as toddlers playing with Tablets and electronic devices

Today, children use laptops for many things, schoolwork, research, projects, reading, and even talking to teachers online. A laptop is not just a toy or an extra gadget. For many children, it is part of their education.

But buying a laptop is not easy. There are many different brands, prices, and technical words that are hard to understand. Many parents feel confused or unsure. They don't want to waste money on the wrong device, and they want to keep their children safe when they go online.

This book is here to help. It is **written in simple English**. You do **not** need to be a computer expert to understand it. You only need to be a parent who wants to make a good decision for your child.

We will talk about:

- How to know if your child really needs a laptop
- The difference between laptops, tablets, and desktop computers
- What parts of a laptop are important (and what is just marketing)
- How to choose a safe and strong laptop for your child
- How to help your child use the laptop in a safe and responsible way

By the end of this book, you will be able to choose the right laptop with **confidence** — not fear.

PART I: UNDERSTANDING THE BASICS

Chapter 1 – Does Your Child Really Need a Laptop?

Why this is important:

Buying a laptop is a big expense. It is good to ask: *"Does my child really need it now?"*

Things to think about:

- **School Requirements:**
  Ask your child's school what they need. Some schools only need children to use shared computers at school. Others may require each child to have their own.
- **Laptop vs. Tablet vs. Desktop:**
  - A **laptop** is portable (can go with your child to school or the library).
  - A **tablet** is lighter and good for reading or watching, but not always good for typing long schoolwork.
  - A **desktop** stays at home, is stronger and cheaper, but not portable.
- **Age and Responsibility:**
  - Younger children can sometimes share a family device.
  - Older children (high school or university) often need their own laptop for daily work.
- **Budget:**
  If money is tight, do not rush. Start with a shared or second-hand device. It is better to plan and buy wisely than to buy fast and regret it later.

Key message:

Not every child needs their own laptop. But if they do, planning first will save money and stress.

Chapter 2 – The Right Age: When Should Kids Get Their Own Laptop?

Why this is important:

Every child grows at a different speed. A laptop can be very useful for school, but it is also a big responsibility. Giving it too early can cause problems. Giving it too late can make schoolwork harder.

This chapter will help you decide **when your child is ready** for their own laptop.

Younger Children (Under 10 Years Old)

- At this age, children are still learning how to read, write, and follow instructions.
- They usually **do not need their own laptop.**
- If they must use a computer, it is better to use a **shared family device** in a public place at home (like the living room).
- They can learn basic skills like:
    - Typing letters
    - Using educational games
    - Watching short learning videos (with a parent watching too)

Tip: Always sit with your child while they use the device. Set a time limit (for example, 30 minutes).

Older Children (10–13 Years Old)

- Children in this age group may start doing **more school projects and online research.**
- They might want their own laptop, but they often still **lack self-control.**
- If you buy a laptop now, use **parental controls** and **time**

limits.

- Teach them:
    - How to search safely
    - How to save their work
    - How to care for the device (charging, cleaning, carrying safely)

Tip: This is a good age to **practice responsibility** before giving them full freedom.

Teenagers (14+ Years Old)

- Teenagers usually **need their own laptop** for school, homework, and preparing for exams or university.
- They need more power (faster laptops with more storage).
- They should also be taught about **online safety, privacy, and digital manners.**
- This is a good time to let them manage their own device — but still check in sometimes.

Tip: Ask them to sign a **"laptop agreement"** about screen time, care, and safe use.

How to Know Your Child Is Ready

Ask yourself these simple questions:

- Can they follow rules?
- Can they keep their things safe?
- Do they understand basic safety (like not talking to strangers online)?
- Do they have a real school need for the laptop?

If the answer is **yes** to most of these, your child may be ready.

Key message:

6

There is no perfect age. The best time is when your child **needs** a laptop for school **and** can use it **responsibly**.

Chapter 3 – Laptop Jargon Made Simple: What Specs Really Matter

Why this is important:

When you shop for a laptop, you will see many confusing words and numbers.

Shops and websites talk about **RAM**, **CPU**, **storage**, **graphics**, and many more.

You don't need to know everything — you only need to know **what really matters** for schoolwork.

This chapter will help you understand the important parts so you can **buy wisely**.

CPU (The Brain)

- The CPU is the **brain** of the laptop.
- It decides how **fast** the computer can think and work.
- Common types: Intel (i3, i5, i7) and AMD (Ryzen 3, 5, 7)

For school:

- Younger children: Intel i3 / Ryzen 3 or better
- Teenagers: Intel i5 / Ryzen 5 or better (faster for many tasks)

Tip: You don't need the most expensive CPU. A mid-range one is enough for school.

◈ **RAM (Short-Term Memory)**

- RAM helps the computer **do many things at once**.
- More RAM = smoother and faster performance.

For school:

- Minimum: 4 GB
- Better: 8 GB
- Best for heavy tasks (video editing, design): 16 GB or more

Tip: For normal schoolwork, 8 GB RAM is perfect.
Storage (Where Files Are Kept)

- Storage is where the laptop **saves all the files, photos, videos, and schoolwork.**
- Two types:
    - HDD (older, slower)
    - SSD (newer, much faster)

For school:

- At least 128 GB SSD (fast and enough for school)
- 256 GB SSD is better if your child will save many videos or photos

Tip: SSD is faster and more reliable than HD
Screen Size

- Small screens (11–13") are light and easy to carry.
- Medium screens (14–15") are good for daily schoolwork.
- Large screens (17") are heavy and not good to carry.

For school:

- 13–14" is a good size — not too big, not too small.

Battery Life

- Important if your child must use the laptop at school without charging.

Look for:

- Battery life of at least 6–8 hours.

Other Useful Features

- **Webcam & microphone:** Needed for online classes.
- **Wi-Fi & Bluetooth:** For internet and connecting to other devices.
- **USB ports & HDMI:** To connect printers, flash drives, or projectors.
- **Strong body:** For younger children, choose a stronger or "rugged" design.

Things You Can Ignore

- Fancy graphics cards (not needed unless your child does gaming or design)
- Very high screen resolution (HD is enough)
- Expensive brand names (focus on performance, not the logo)

Key message:
Focus on **CPU, RAM, storage, battery life, and screen size.**
These 5 things will help your child do their schoolwork smoothly — without wasting money.

Chapter 4 – Operating Systems Explained: Windows, macOS, or Chrome OS?

Why this is important:

Every laptop uses an **operating system (OS)**.

The OS is like the **manager** of the computer. It controls how the laptop works and what programs you can use.

The three most common operating systems are:

Windows, macOS, and Chrome OS.

Each has good points and weak points.

This chapter will help you choose the one that fits your child's needs.

Windows (Microsoft)

What it is:

- The most popular system in the world
- Used on many different brands (HP, Lenovo, Dell, Acer, etc.)

Good points:

- Works with almost all school software
- Easy to find help or repair
- Wide choice of prices and models

Weak points:

- Can be slow on very cheap laptops
- Needs good antivirus protection

Best for:

General school use, older children, and teenagers who need many types of programs.

macOS (Apple)

What it is:

- Only used on Apple laptops (MacBook)

Good points:

- Very fast and smooth
- Long-lasting and good battery life
- Less risk of viruses

Weak points:

- Expensive
- Repairs can cost a lot
- Not all school software works on macOS

Best for:

Older students who do creative work (art, music, video, design) and can take care of expensive equipment.

Chrome OS (Google)

What it is:

- Used on Chromebooks (small, simple laptops)
- Mostly works online using the internet

Good points:

- Very simple and fast
- Long battery life
- Usually cheap

Weak points:

- Needs internet to do most things

- Not good for heavy work (video editing, coding)
- Small storage space

Best for:

Younger children and basic schoolwork like writing, reading, and browsing the web.

Quick Comparison Table

Feature	Windows	macOS	Chrome OS
Price range	Low to high	High only	Low
Easy to use	Medium	Easy	Very easy
Battery life	Medium	Long	Long
Works offline	Yes	Yes	Limited
School software	Almost all	Most	Only basic

Key message:

Choose the system that fits your child's **age, school needs, and your budget.**

- Chrome OS is simple and cheap for younger kids.
- Windows is flexible and works for most students.
- macOS is powerful but expensive — better for older students who need it.

PART II: CHOOSING WISELY

Chapter 5 – Budgeting Without Compromising

Why this is important:

Laptops can be expensive, and prices can confuse parents.

A high price does **not** always mean good quality, and a low price does **not** always mean poor quality.

This chapter will help you **understand what to expect at different price levels** so you can buy the best laptop for your money.

Under $300 (Basic Budget)

What you get:

- Small, light laptops or Chromebooks
- Simple performance (good for typing, browsing, reading)
- Usually 4 GB RAM, 64–128 GB storage
- Often plastic body, not very strong

Good for:

- Young children who only do simple tasks
- Basic schoolwork (reading, writing, online lessons)

Be careful:

- Not very fast with many apps open
- May not last many years
- Sometimes short battery life

Around $500 (Mid-range Budget)

What you get:

- Faster laptops with better build quality
- Usually 8 GB RAM, 128–256 GB SSD
- Better screens and longer battery life
- Good webcam and microphone

Good for:

- Older children and teenagers
- Daily homework, video calls, presentations, light photo editing

Best value:

- This price range gives **good balance** of power and price.

Around $1000 (High Budget)
What you get:

- Fast and powerful laptops (Intel i5/i7, Ryzen 5/7)
- 16 GB RAM or more, 512 GB or more storage
- Strong design, long battery life, very smooth performance

Good for:

- High school and university students
- Heavy tasks like video editing, coding, or design

Be careful:

- Very expensive to repair if broken
- Only buy if your child really needs this power

Refurbished or Second-hand Laptops
What it means:

Used laptops that have been cleaned, repaired, and checked by sellers.

Good points:

- Much cheaper
- Good for short-term use
- Can be enough for simple school tasks

Be careful:

- Check battery life and warranty
- Make sure it is not too old (less than 5 years is safer)

Tips to Save Money

- Ask the school if they give student discounts.
- Compare prices online before you buy.
- Avoid paying extra for brand names or fancy looks.
- Focus on what your child needs, not on what looks popular.

Key message:

You don't need to buy the most expensive laptop.

Choose the **price range that matches your child's needs** and **your family's budget**.

A smart choice now saves money later.

PART II: CHOOSING WISELY

Chapter 6 – Durability, Portability & Battery Life

Why this is important:

Children carry laptops to school, libraries, and friends' houses.

A laptop that is too heavy, too weak, or with poor battery life will cause problems.

This chapter will help you choose a laptop that is **strong, easy to carry, and lasts all day.**

Durability (How Strong It Is)

Children are not always careful — accidents happen.

Look for:

- Strong body (metal or hard plastic)
- Spill-resistant keyboard (helps if water or juice is dropped)
- Shock protection (some laptops are made for schools and can survive drops)

Tips:

- Buy a **good padded laptop bag or sleeve**
- Add a **screen protector** if possible
- Teach your child how to carry it with two hands

Key message: A strong laptop lasts longer and saves repair money.

Portability (Easy to Carry)

If the laptop is too big or heavy, your child will not want to carry it to school.

Look for:

- Weight under 1.5 kg (light enough for daily travel)
- Medium size screen (13–14 inches is perfect)
- Slim design that fits into a school bag

Avoid:

- Very large 17" laptops — they are heavy and hard to carry

Key message: A small, light laptop is easier to carry and safer for children.

Battery Life (How Long It Lasts)

School days are long, and not every classroom has a charger nearby.

Look for:

- Battery life of at least 6–8 hours
- Fast charging if possible
- Reviews that mention "good battery life"

Tips:

- Teach your child to **charge the laptop every night**
- Turn down screen brightness to save power

Key message: A long battery life means less stress and no empty battery during class.

Summary

- **Younger children:** Choose a small, light, strong laptop
- **Teenagers:** Choose a light laptop with long battery life and enough power
- Always protect the laptop with a good bag and teach safe handling

Final Thought:

A laptop for school should be **strong enough to survive, light enough to carry, and powerful enough to last through the day.**

Chapter 7 – Safety First: What Every Parent Should Look For

Why this is important:

When you buy a laptop for your child, you are not just buying a machine — you are opening a **door to the internet.**

That door can lead to **great learning**, but also to **dangers** like viruses, scams, and harmful content.

This chapter will show you how to **keep your child safe** and **protect the laptop** at the same time.

Protecting Your Child Online

Parental Controls

- Many laptops have **built-in parental control settings.**
- You can block harmful websites, limit screen time, and control what apps can be installed.
- On Windows: use **Microsoft Family Safety**
- On macOS: use **Screen Time**
- On Chromebooks: use **Google Family Link**

Tip: Set up parental controls **before giving the laptop to your child.**

Safe Browsing

- Teach your child to only visit **safe, trusted websites.**
- Explain that they should **never talk to strangers online** or share personal details (like name, school, or address).
- Encourage them to **ask you** if they see something strange or scary.

Online Privacy

- Show your child how to use **strong passwords.**
- Use **separate accounts** for each family member on the laptop.
- Turn off the **webcam** when not in use (you can even cover it with tape or a webcam cover).

Protecting the Laptop Itself
Antivirus Protection

- Install a **reliable antivirus program** (many are free or low-cost).
- It protects the laptop from viruses, malware, and hackers.
- Keep it **updated regularly.**

Automatic Updates

- Turn on **automatic updates** for the system and software.
- This keeps the laptop safe from new security risks.

Backups

- Help your child **save their schoolwork in the cloud** (like Google Drive or OneDrive).
- If the laptop breaks, they will not lose their work.

Physical Safety

- Use a **strong case or laptop bag** to prevent drops and bumps.
- Teach your child:
    - Don't eat or drink near the laptop
    - Don't leave it on the floor
    - Always close it gently

What NOT to Buy

- Laptops with **no webcam privacy cover** (easy to fix by buying a cover)
- Very **cheap no-name brands** with no warranty or support
- Devices with **short battery life** or **no parental control options**

Key message:

Safety comes first — **protect your child online and protect the laptop from damage.**

A safe laptop gives you peace of mind and gives your child a safe space to learn.

PART III: RESPONSIBLE USE & SETUP

Chapter 8 – Setting Up the Laptop Safely

Why this is important:

When you buy a new laptop, it is like getting a blank notebook — you must **set it up correctly** before your child starts using it.

A safe and clean setup helps keep the laptop **fast, safe, and ready for learning.**

This chapter will give you **easy steps** to follow.

Step 1 – Create a User Account for Your Child

- Every laptop lets you create **separate user accounts.**
- This helps keep their work private and stops them from changing important settings.

How to do it:

- **Windows:** Settings → Accounts → Family & other users
- **macOS:** System Settings → Users & Groups
- **Chromebook:** Add your child using Google Family Link

Tip: Use your own account as **Administrator** and your child's as **Standard User**.

This prevents them from installing unwanted apps.

Step 2 – Install Security Protection

- Install a **good antivirus program** to block viruses and malware.
- Turn on the **built-in firewall** (this stops hackers).
- Set the system to **update automatically** so it stays safe.

Optional but helpful:

- Install **ad blockers** in the browser to stop harmful pop-ups.
- Use **child-friendly browsers** (like Google Kids Space or Kiddle for younger kids).

Step 3 – Set Up Parental Controls

- Parental controls help you:
    - Block harmful websites
    - Limit screen time
    - See what your child is doing

Tools to use:

- Windows: Microsoft Family Safety
- macOS: Screen Time
- Chromebook: Google Family Link

Tip: Explain to your child that this is **for safety, not punishment.**
Step 4 – Turn On Backups

- Backups save your child's schoolwork in case the laptop breaks.

Easy backup options:

- Google Drive (works on all systems)
- Microsoft OneDrive
- Apple iCloud (on Macs)

Tip: Ask your child to save schoolwork in the cloud every day.
Step 5 – Install Useful Learning Tools

- Web browser (Chrome, Edge, Safari)

- Office tools (Microsoft Office, Google Docs)
- PDF reader
- Dictionary or translation apps
- School software your school recommends

Step 6 – Teach the Basics

Show your child how to:

- Log in with their password
- Save and find their files
- Charge the laptop safely
- Close programs when they are done

Key message:

A safe setup protects your child and the laptop.
It also makes the laptop ready for learning from the very first day.

PART III: RESPONSIBLE USE & SETUP

Chapter 9 – Teaching Tech Responsibility

Why this is important:
Giving a laptop to your child is not only about schoolwork — it also teaches them **independence and responsibility.**

Without clear rules, they might spend too much time playing games, watching videos, or visiting unsafe websites.

This chapter will help you guide your child to use technology **wisely and safely.**

Set Clear Time Limits

- Too much screen time can harm your child's eyes, sleep, and focus.
- Children need time to play outside, talk to people, and rest.

Tips:

- For younger children (under 10): about 1 hour per day
- For older children and teens: 2–3 hours (schoolwork time not included)
- Use parental control tools to set daily limits

Tip: Make a **screen time schedule** and stick to it.

Teach Focus and Good Study Habits

- Help your child use the laptop **only for schoolwork during homework time.**
- Ask them to **close all games and social media** while studying.
- Teach them to work in a **quiet, clean place** with good light.

Useful habits:

- Take a 5-minute break every 30 minutes
- Save their work often
- Finish tasks before opening games or videos

Teach Digital Safety and Etiquette

- Explain that **everything they post online can be seen by others.**
- Teach them:
    - Be kind and respectful online
    - Never send personal photos or private information to strangers
    - Tell you if they see something strange, scary, or rude online

Golden Rule:
"If you wouldn't say it face to face, don't say it online."
Teach Laptop Care

- Always carry the laptop with two hands
- Don't eat or drink near it
- Keep it in a safe place when not in use
- Charge it every night

Tip: Make your child responsible for keeping their device clean and charged.
Be a Good Example

- Children copy what they see.
- If you also use your phone or laptop responsibly, they will too.
- Try to have **tech-free family times** (like during meals).

Key message:

Teaching your child to be responsible is just as important as giving them the laptop.

Good habits now will help them become **safe, respectful, and balanced digital citizens.**

PART III: RESPONSIBLE USE & SETUP

Chapter 10 – Ongoing Maintenance and Support

(H*ow to keep the laptop healthy — and what to do when things go wrong)*

Why this is important:

A laptop is like a bicycle or a car — it works well if you **take care of it regularly**.

Without care, it can become slow, break, or lose important files.

This chapter will show you how to **keep the laptop working** and **handle problems calmly.**

Keep the Laptop Clean and Fast

Physical cleaning

- Wipe the screen and keyboard gently with a soft dry cloth
- Never use water or strong cleaners
- Keep food and drinks away from the laptop

Digital cleaning

- Delete old or unused files and apps
- Empty the Recycle Bin/Trash every few weeks
- Clear browser history and cookies (helps websites load faster)

Tip: Do this together with your child every month — it teaches good habits.

Keep the Software Updated

- Turn on **automatic system updates**
- Update apps and antivirus programs regularly

- Updates fix problems and make the laptop safer

Tip: Restart the laptop after updates so they can finish installing.

Back Up Important Files

- Save schoolwork in cloud storage (Google Drive, OneDrive, iCloud)
- Keep copies of important files on a USB drive or external hard drive

Tip: This protects schoolwork if the laptop breaks or gets lost.

When Something Goes Wrong

If the laptop is slow:

- Restart it
- Close unused programs
- Check for updates
- Run an antivirus scan

If the laptop freezes:

- Hold the power button to turn it off
- Wait 10 seconds
- Turn it back on

If the internet does not work:

- Restart the Wi-Fi router
- Check if other devices can connect
- Ask your internet provider for help

If it breaks or won't start:

- Do not try to fix it yourself

- Take it to a repair shop or ask the seller (if it's still under warranty)

Tip: Stay calm — most problems can be fixed easily.

When to Upgrade or Replace

- The laptop is more than 5–6 years old and very slow
- It cannot run the new school software
- Repairs cost more than buying a new one
- The battery no longer lasts even 1 hour

Remember:

Upgrading (like adding more RAM or a new battery) is sometimes cheaper than buying new.

Key message:

A little care will make a laptop last many years.

If something goes wrong, don't panic — follow simple steps or ask for help.

This teaches your child how to **solve problems calmly and responsibly.**

www.ingramcontent.com/pod-product-compliance
Lightning Source LLC
LaVergne TN
LVHW022325200926
848481LV00004B/1438
* 9 7 9 8 2 3 2 3 5 8 9 1 4 *